and father are gone. But I don't want to think about that.

Or when the man threatened me with a knife and stole my pack. My pack, with my phone . . . my phone, and my papers.

My phone, full of photos of my sisters and mum and dad, and my friends, their numbers – videos, playlists, all the fun things from my life.

And the papers – papers which would let everybody know for certain that today is my birthday, and mum and dad's full names, the name of our village, and everything about me, my story, all the stuff that I am beginning to forget.

Which is why nobody here knows it is my birthday. So nobody here gives me any presents.

If anybody gave me a birthday card, I would show it to the Guards, and say, *Hey, look! Do you believe me now? My name! My age! Here on my birthday card! Proof!*

This is why I want to tell you my story, because the Guards say that everything that happens must be *documented*.

But I'm not going to tell the story of my past. I'm going to tell the story of my life right now, here in the Camp, beginning today.

On my tenth birthday.

My story goes like this . . .

I

My friends, L and E, are crouching down in the mud, picking breadcrumbs. L is rolling the pieces into small balls, adding crumbs as she shuffles along, adding and rolling, then carefully placing the bread patties into a plastic bag hooked round her wrist.

E has a carrier bag around his wrist as well, but he sneaks most of the crumbs into his mouth as he picks them, and the balls he is rolling don't really hold together. He is making a mess.

E is wearing trousers that have been donated and are too big for him, rolled up at the cuffs so they don't drag in the mud, and baggy round the waist. They make him look even smaller than he is, and he is pretty tiny to begin with. His sister L has grown too big for her own clothes, and the sleeves on her jumper only reach halfway to her wrists. L and E look silly, crouched in the mud, too big and too small.

At first I think they are picking brown breadcrumbs, but when I get closer I see the bread has been soaking up the mud water, like gravy.

'Who wants to play?' I say.

E springs to his feet. 'Meee!'

'We're eating,' says L. 'Look,' she says. 'Look at all this food.'

'For real?' I say.

'When the aid truck came,' L says, 'everybody made a mad rush and grabbed all the bread. It was gone before me and E could get anywhere near. But look,' – she spreads her hands across the mud in front of her – 'they wasted all of this. Dropped a zillion crumbs and just left them. It's treasure.'

'What shall we play?' E asks me, popping crumbs into his mouth as he speaks.

'Don't eat them all now.' L tsks at her little brother. 'You'll have none left for later.'

'I know where there's apples,' I say.

Her head jerks up. 'What?'

'Apples!' I say. '*Juicy* apples. But only for secret agents.'

'Not kids then,' says L, looking back down.

She is grumpy today.

'I'm only messing,' I say. 'But there *are* apples.'

'I'm a secret agent,' says E. 'Can I have an apple?'

'I'm *head* secret agent,' I say.

'I'm head secret agent,' says E.

'You can't both be the head secret agent,' says L. 'Anyway, if anyone's a secret agent, I'm a secret agent.'

'That's stupid,' says E. 'You can't be a secret agent because secret agents are men.'

'And you two are little boys,' says L. 'I'm the oldest, so if anybody is a secret agent then it's me. And anyway, I'm the leader.'

You're still a little child though, I think. *You're not* that *much older than me. And I'm only ten.*

'But you don't know where the apples are,'
I say.

'Show me,' she says, 'and I'll keep us safe.'

L will keep us safe?

E picks up a twig. 'I've got a gun,' he says.
'It's a rifle.'

I pick up E's carrier bag and hook the
handles over my ears, so the bag hangs behind
my neck. 'And I've got a cloak of invisibility.
Come on, let's go.'

So off we go, to search for the apples, L, E and I.

'Secret agents don't have a cloak of invisibility,'
says L. 'You're thinking of wizards.'

'This wizard just joined the secret service,'
I say. 'Are you a witch?'

She doesn't answer. She grabs E by the collar and at the same time gives me a shove so hard I fall into a bush, and I scratch my arm.

'What was that for?' I ask her.

'Shush.'

I peek through the leaves of the bush and I see a Guard. He has a real rifle, and has stopped on the path ahead of us. L is holding E down close to the ground and has her finger to his lips so he won't make any noise.

We are on the edge of the administration zone. Only Guards are allowed in this area.

E holds up his twig. 'Shall I shoot him?' he whispers.

I wonder if the Guard would shoot *us*. I have never heard of a Guard shooting any of the children. But they have clubs. Once, when everybody gathered to ask for blankets when the snow came, a Guard struck me on the arm and my bruise changed colour every day for a week. It was like a slow motion rainbow.

The Guard's club is a hundred times thicker than E's twig.

'Why didn't you tell us the apples were in the administration zone?' L hisses.

'Did you think they'd just be hanging on a tree?' I ask.

She doesn't answer that.

The Guard passes by and doesn't see us hiding behind the bush. I still have E's carrier bag hooked on my ears. 'The invisibility cloak worked!' I give L and E the thumbs up.

'Which way from here?' says L.

'The smoking patch.'

The smoking patch is outside the admin block, where the Guards go to smoke their cigarettes. Hardly anybody in the Camp smokes, not even the grown-ups. Everybody needs food, and warmth. Smoking is of no use. But the Guards must have plenty of food, because they never look hungry, or skinny, and they waste their time putting cigarettes in their mouths and puffing smoke.

And they waste food. If they can afford to waste food, then they must be getting plenty of it. Which makes me wonder why they keep it all to themselves. Which makes me wonder why they won't let any of us out of the Camp to try and find food of our own. I wonder about that a lot.

'Shall we tunnel?' says E.

'No,' says L. 'But we'll crawl. We'll crawl through the long grass. On our bellies. Like secret agents on a surprise attack, remember?'

'Spies,' says E. 'Do or die.'

The grass tickles my nose.

We crawl all the way to the smoking patch without being seen. It's easier not being seen when you're a kid.

'I'm a cat,' I say, 'sneaking up on a bird.'

'I'm a tiger,' says E, 'hunting a monkey.'

'Shush!' says L. There is a Guard standing ahead, puffing on his cigarette. L is worried about us getting caught.

But I'm not worried. If children in the Camp get caught breaking any of the rules, then their families get sanctions. Sanctions is another word for punishment, where you get sent to the back of the queue. The reason I'm not worried about my family getting punished is because I lost my family. Or my family lost me. L and E don't have any family either because they all got blown up.

And we're not even *in* the queue are we, so how could we be sent to the back of it? If they put us at the back of the queue, it would be brilliant, like a *reward*.

So when I see the Guard, I stay *shush* like L says, but only because I remember the rainbow bruise on my arm.

He is standing by a litter bin but he throws

the cigarette stub on the ground. There are loads of stubs scattered on the ground.

'I don't see any apples,' says L.

'Wait,' I say.

The Guard looks around. I wonder if he has heard us. But then I realise he's not really looking around. His job is to smoke cigarettes and look around. Now that he has smoked his cigarette he is doing the looking around bit.

Job done, I imagine him saying to himself. He turns around and walks back towards the building.

'Bang!' says E, shooting the Guard in the back with his twig.

'Shush!' says L. But the Guard is already making his way through the door.

'You missed,' I say to E, who's blowing the rifle smoke from the end of his twig.

I stand up.

'What are you doing?' L hisses.

'Watch.' I walk right up to the bin. I hear E gasp behind me. E likes to play at being brave, but he's only little, and he never sees L being brave because it is L's job to be careful. Her job is to look after her little brother. If she gets into trouble because of playing at being brave, and she gets separated from him, E won't have anybody left. He'll be all on his own.

And little kids like E, when they are left all on their own, they disappear. They get taken.

It is why we must all stick together. To watch out for each other.

I am standing on the concrete next to the bin. I wave at L and E. She ducks further down behind the bush, and pulls E down with her. It's like hide-and-seek.

I shove my arm down into the bin, and I feel around. My fingers brush against something sticky, which I think is an old wrapper. Then they brush against something soft and warm, which I think is an old rag one of the Guards used for cleaning mud from his boots. Then they brush against the little twig that sticks up out of the top of an apple. The stalk. I tweezer it between my finger and thumb, and pull it out. There are two more in here too – I saw the Guards drop them in earlier, when I was spying.

I pick all three apples out of the bin and

hurry with them back to the bush. L and E hold out their hands eagerly.

L frowns. 'There's not much to them, is there?' she says.

But E says, 'This is amazing!' He starts crunching into his apple straight away.

They are both right. I gave the biggest apple core to E because he is the littlest, and I gave L the smallest apple core, because she is the biggest. I kept the middle-sized one for myself. It is pretty chunky. L is right about how much people waste. The Guards won't eat the core of the apple because it has pips and isn't so juicy – but here I am munching away at half an apple. I don't even bother spitting the pips, because pips are good for you too. It may not be the juiciest part of the apple, but it is still pretty lush.

'This is a feast!' says E. He is grinning and chewing both at the same time.

'Don't talk with your mouth full,' L tells him. But she is smiling too, and I know I've done well. This is a million times better than muddy old breadcrumbs.

Happy Birthday, I think.

L, I, E

The Camp is not what most people think of as camping. People come on day trips, bringing us gifts of food or clean clothes. You should see the look on their faces – like the world exploded.

Charity told me that whenever she invites friends along to the Camp for their first time, they expect it to look like a holiday camp. Imagine that! Charity is a volunteer who has visited us at the Camp so many times that she lives here now too. I think it's weird, because everybody in the Camp is desperate to get out of it, but Charity chooses to come into the Camp, and decides to stay. The last time she came to the Camp, she arrived in a double-decker bus. She parked it on the ridge of the hill and said, 'This is the centre for women and children.'

L told me that there needs to be a space especially for women and children because women who are on their own do not feel safe. And unaccompanied minors are the least safe of all. I'm an unaccompanied minor. Except I'm not really unaccompanied. I'm with L and E. They're my company. I suppose by unaccompanied they mean unaccompanied by grown-ups. And that is true. Some of the children and women who are on their own sleep on the double-decker with Charity. They have safety in numbers, and *Men Are Not Allowed.*

You still see plenty of kids wandering around on their own though, at all times of day.

Some of the families in the Camp live in big metal boxes. I've seen them. Big metal boxes with doors and bunk beds inside. They remind me of many years ago, before all of this. My sister made a dolls' house from an old shoebox and put little matchboxes in it and pretended they were beds for her dolls. Her worry dolls. You put your worries to bed, see?

I can remember that.

But that was then, and the big metal boxes are now. I wouldn't fancy sleeping in one myself, but in any case they're only for families, or groups. Unaccompanied minors like me wouldn't be safe in a big metal box.

I live in a wooden shed with L and E. It doesn't have any water, or light, or heat, and sometimes the rats get in, but it's better than a tent. We found a mat buried in sludge in the ditch and hung it up to dry. The sludge went crusty and we beat the mat until it turned to dust and blew away. The mat turned from brown to red and we laid it on the floor with a crate on it, wrong way up, and stuck a candle on top. It's like a home. At night we padlock the door and it is not bad.

We're going there now, because I've got a surprise. A birthday surprise.

'Who wants to play?' I ask.

E jumps up and down. 'Me! Me! Me! Me!'

I thought so.

I stole a thread from Charity's blanket.

Well, first I found the plastic action figures. I was rummaging down in the ditch, looking for more things for the shed, and I found a plastic soldier, and a plastic Roman gladiator and a plastic doctor. The Guards try and stop the children from digging around in the ditch because it's where the waste goes – people's torn clothes or broken seats or bent spoons; but also rotten food and bits of dead birds and icky stuff like that, but that's only really in Deep Ditch. The part of the ditch that's on higher ground is mainly odd bits, and that's where I found the plastic figures. The figures are about the same size as my sister's worry dolls but they're much more real because they are made from plastic rather than old pegs.

So I found my soldier and my gladiator and my doctor and I borrowed three threads from Charity's blanket. It's the blanket she always wraps round herself to keep warm. I mean I didn't tear the thread out of the blanket. Her blanket is always unravelling. The threads are all different colours and keep getting wrapped up in things. Charity once gave me a cheese sandwich and it had one of her blanket threads in it. When I pulled it out it was about two feet long! In fact, that was one of the ones I took.

I tied one end of the blanket thread round the soldier's head, and the other end around the end of a twig. And I did the same with the gladiator and the doctor. When you jerk the twig they dance, or fly, or run, or fight. You can make them do anything.

It is my birthday, so I am giving gifts to my friends. Mum always used to say, *to give is to receive.* So, if you think of it like that, these are my birthday presents.

E loves them. Straight away he grabs the gladiator, who has a spear and a metal helmet, and he sets the figure racing through the mud,

hunting for beetles or worms. 'Stab! Stab! Stab!'
he shrieks. 'Stab! Stab! Stab!'

I give L the doctor.

'How come I get the doctor?' she says, pulling
her offended face.

I know better than to argue. I give her the
soldier. I take the doctor, and I wait for the
gladiator or the soldier to shoot or stab the other
one, and then I shall airlift them to safety. Or
bury them.

The soldier jumps on the gladiator's head.
'Bang! You're dead!' yells L. See?

I decide the doctor is going to punch the
soldier on the nose and strangle him with
his stethoscope.

'My gladiator fires lightning bolts!' says E.

The strings get all tangled and we're having a tug of death, when from up the hill we hear yelling and shrieking and shouting. We drop our twigs.

'V,' says L.

Of course it's V. It's always V. What's she up to this time?

We race up the hill. There is a crowd gathered and they are watching V. They are watching V wrestle with a Guard's leg. They are listening to V shriek. V can howl like a wolf, trumpet like an elephant, laugh like a hyena and hiss like a cat. Right now, she sounds like she's doing all of them at the same time.

She is hooked, half upside down, round a

Guard's leg and is tugging at his boot. The Guard is trying to shake her off but she's clinging like a monkey. Other Guards are trying to grab at her but when they get too close she scratches out at them.

'V!' yells L. 'V! Stop it!'

V is not wearing any shoes. One of her socks is hanging off where one of the Guards tried to pull her away. That has made her really mad because V takes a lot of care about how she's dressed. She wears a sports top and tracksuit bottoms, so she always looks like she's about to run a race – and go for gold.

'She's going to be in big trouble, isn't she?' says E.

I don't answer him. I mean, V can't really

be in trouble, can she? What are they going to do – lock her up? We're already locked up. What else are they going to do – throw her out of the Camp? V's been trying to escape from the Camp since forever.

But they might hurt her. Some of the Guards are laughing, but I see one of them pulling out his club.

'L,' I say, 'do something.'

But what can L do? About the only thing she has in common with V is that they're both girls. L's got more sense though – she has to, because E needs her to do things right.

'Don't, V,' L says. 'Don't, or they'll hurt you!'

See? As if the human hurricane that is V is going to take any notice of that.

Then, all at once, V's got the Guard's boot wrenched off his foot. She holds it up above her head like a prize. 'Hah ha!' she yells, jumping up and down. 'Mine!'

She starts running away with the Guard's boot.

If the Guards have to chase after her, they will beat her when they catch her.

None of the grown-ups look as if they want to get involved. When you've been clubbed once, it is not something you rush into twice.

So I throw myself in front of her path. V is really skinny, like everybody in Camp, but she says she's almost sixteen. She is at least a foot taller than me, and sends me flying.

But I managed to wrap myself round her legs,

so V goes flying too, and we're both all a tangle in the mud. The boot scuttles out of her hands and rolls away. The Guard picks it up and shoves his foot back into it, scowling at us.

The other Guards applaud. They think it is funny.

'Are you crazy?' I say to V.

She pushes me off of her and stands with her hands on her hips in front of the Guard. She points a finger at his face.

'He stole my shoes.'

The accusation hangs in the air, while we all think about it. The Guards just stand there, waiting to see what happens next, whether they need to hit us.

'Well?' one of the grown-ups says to the Guard.

'Yes,' the Guard admits. 'We confiscated Child V's shoes. Hers, and the other two who were going walkabout – Child Y and Child B.'

This is what they call us – Child L, Child E, etc., etc., etc. Because we can't prove our real names.

I am Child I.

'See?' says V.

'You can't do that,' I shout.

'Thief!' yells V.

'Her and her mates were on the railway track,' says the Guard. 'We have a duty of care.'

'We slipped out of the gates,' V grins at me. 'Me and two others. We were going to catch a train.'

'If an unaccompanied minor is putting

themselves at risk,' the Guard continues, 'we can use any reasonable means to maintain their safety.'

'My shoes!' yells V.

'Including the removal of footwear, if the minor is making use of the footwear to trespass on dangerous ground.'

'But you can't take her shoes,' says one of the grown-ups. 'How is she going to get around Camp?'

The Guard shrugs.

'You have no right to keep me here,' shouts V. 'I have an auntie who's going to take me in. I've got rights.'

'It's true,' I say. 'I've seen the photos. V's told us all about it. Her auntie lives in a big house and she has loads of money, and she has promised to pay for V and everything.'

The Guards are standing in a line with their arms crossed.

'And who has Child V shared this story with?' asks the Guard in charge. He won't speak to V herself, I suppose because he thinks she looks too wild to talk to. She is walking round in tight little circles, muttering to herself, with her fists raised like she's going to do two rounds in a boxing ring. 'Has it been corroborated?'

'Corrobawhatwhat?' says E, squinching his face up at me.

'The Guard wants to know if V can prove it,' I translate for him.

'The Guard thinks V may be lying,' adds L.

'It's not a lie!' V yells. She rushes up to the Guard, pushing her chin at his face. The other Guards put their hands to their clubs.

'It's *not* a lie,' I back her up. 'She shouldn't be here.'

'All right,' says the Guard. And he finally locks eyes with V. He holds out his hand. 'Passport?'

V's passport. Her *Life Book*.

She doesn't have one. Somebody stole V's Life Book, and this is her trouble. Without her Life Book, everything V says might be one big lie.

Here in the Camp we call your passport your Life Book. Without it, you have no life. For starters, you can't prove that you are who you say you are. You could be called anything. V says her auntie lives in a pretty village with her husband who is a dentist. V's auntie and her husband even visited the Camp, and they spoke to V and gave her some food and clothes (they gave her the shoes that the Guard just stole!).

They spoke to the man in the administration zone and told him all about how V's mum and dad were shot by some soldiers, and how V fled with her older brother. How they travelled in a boat and the boat sank because there were too many passengers. V's brother drowned, and now she is on her own.

Except she is not on her own. She has her auntie, her rich auntie in the pretty village. But V lost her passport in the sea along with her brother, so none of it matters. The man in the administration zone says Child V's story could be one big lie. And without her passport she can't even prove that she *is* V. And they won't believe her auntie, because her auntie could be lying too.

It's no wonder V's so mad all the time. She's off the map.

You need your passport in order to pass through the ports from one country into another. That's the problem. It tells the whole story of your life – your name, your birthday, your parents' names, where you live, where you've been, and a picture of your face. Your whole life, on separate leaves of paper, bound together into one important book – your Life Book.

And most importantly of all, when they take your picture to put in your Life Book, you *must not smile.* If you smile, then your Life Book won't be allowed. You have to show people that you have a sad life.

I want my life to be happy. My Life Book should be full of pictures of me smiling – smiling at my family and friends, all gathered around the camera, calling out, 'Smile!'

I lost my Life Book too. Most of the unaccompanied minors in the Camp lost their Life Books. They have been stolen, or seized, or bombed, or burnt, or drowned.

This is why I have to tell my story. L's and E's and V's as well. If no one will listen to our stories we will never get out of this place. We will never find ourselves a new home. We will never have new stories and live more life.

V's socks are covered in dirt and she's worn holes in the heels already from stomping around. I'm worried she's going to jump on one of the Guards again. E is watching her and watching the Guards. He looks like he is going to cry.

L reaches into her plastic food bag and says to V, 'Look, I made a breadcrumb pattie. Would you like it?'

E straight away focuses on the pattie. He's like a hungry doggie, even though he's already eaten his share of the breadcrumbs, and the apple core too. V reaches out and takes the breadcrumb pattie. Her eyes narrow and a sly look crosses her face. I think for a second she's going to throw the pattie at the Guard who stole her shoes. But she seems to change her mind and shoves it into her mouth, mud and all.

E can't hide his look of disappointment. For some reason he thinks every pattie has got his name on it.

I have an idea. I skip forward and smile.

'Who wants to play?' I say.

The Camp had a youth club that was built by a group of volunteers. It had ping-pong and table football and other good stuff. But the men who built it decided that it was a youth club only for boys, which meant that L and V weren't able to go in. I enjoyed it though. You got free snacks and they also had card games and music.

Then, for some reason, the Guards decided the youth club was a breach of the rules because the people who built it hadn't asked for permission, so they smashed it up. What a waste!

But it worked out well for the girls, because Charity got hold of the table football, and she keeps it safe at night in the women and children's bus. Then, during the day, it gets carried out onto the road, and anyone can play it – boys *and* girls.

L told me that the women and children's bus will never get demolished like the youth club because you can't demolish a double-decker bus. You can only move it on. And the bus can keep driving around different parts of the

Camp whenever any of the Guards say it's got to move. And it will never be towed away because what tow truck is big enough to tow away a double-decker?

So L and I play V and E at table football and V takes out her mood on the spinning players. We get whupped six goals to nil, even though E can't really see over the edge of the table to spin his players. V plays like her life depends on it. Pretty soon I think she's forgotten how angry she is at the shoe-stealing Guard because she's scored all six goals and is skipping around whooping and pumping the air and yelling, 'Champions!' She makes the L-shape with her finger and thumb and shouts, 'Looo-sers!' at L and me.

She's not a very nice winner, V. None of us mind, because it's good to see her smiling again. Also, I had a second reason for bringing us to the children's bus, as well as playing football. Charity has a box full of shoes donated by people who have heard about our situation. There's bound to be a pair that fit V.

And there is! When Charity brings out the shoebox, word has already spread, and there is a mad scrum for shoes, mostly big men who live in the Camp, pushing everyone else aside. But V has mastered the art of ducking between people's legs. She is fast too, and doesn't mind using her elbows against men who are twice her size.

V comes out triumphant, clutching a pair of

Adidas that aren't too scrubby. She is grinning ear to ear and really does look like she's bouncing on air.

I am tired by the time we get back to our shed.

V has taken her own way to the women and children's bus, where Charity tells me she sleeps at the back of the upper deck, wrapped up in a duvet. 'Like a fox,' says Charity, 'snuggled up in her den.'

I picture V as I snuggle myself into my sleeping bag, thinking my eyes will close in two seconds flat. But I find myself looking across at L and E. They sleep together in a pile of old blankets. Every night L brings out a big photo album.

She told me how she and E arrived here after walking through miles of countryside on their own, hiding behind hedges to avoid strangers, eating whatever they could find, and sheltering in barns or under trees. Once, they were robbed and the men took everything they had, which wasn't much. Some clothes, a couple of forks, their plastic macs. The thieves wanted to take their photo album too, and L begged them not to. L promised herself to keep it safe and carry it with her wherever they travelled.

Now, in the quiet of our shack she opens the album out across the top of the blanket. She points at the faces in the pictures, naming friends, family, and remembering the past.

'See?' says L to E. 'Remember who this

is – our uncle from Mama's old village, with his bird's-nest beard?'

E stares at the picture, but he says nothing. He just blinks. As if he cannot remember. Or as if he does not wish to remember.

I remember my own uncle with his own bird's-nest beard, the look on his face as he lifted me onto the boat, the last time I saw him. But sometimes I wish I could just forget.

Sometimes I wish I could make myself forget, like E.

L hugs E close, with the album spread over both their knees. She is stroking his arm. She hums a tune to him, a lullaby.

Every night I watch L guide E through the picture book, the only sound in our shack,

E falling asleep in her arms. And then I fall asleep smiling.

The next morning we go meet V on the bus, hoping for breakfast. Today, there is no breakfast. E is all grumbly and moany. L and I try and cheer him. We try and touch our noses with the tips of our tongues – which L can actually do! V doesn't join in. She sits quietly, and I imagine her thinking about her auntie's house, and hot cooked breakfast in her auntie's kitchen.

'It won't be long now,' she tells me, 'before I get there.'

But I'm not so sure. I mean, it's already been *long* hasn't it?

Then, everything gets better! V comes with

us as we make our way through the Camp –
part of me thinks it's so we can all hunt for
food together, but a bigger part of me hopes
it's actually because she wants to be part of our
gang – and we find a real piece of treasure. E
digs it out of one of the mountains of rubbish
that are growing up all over the Camp. A giant
rubber ring! It's the kind that people use when
they are playing on a beach, bobbing along in
the surf in the sunshine. I don't know what it's
doing here, in the Camp. It has a puncture, of
course, and is covered in brown smears. At
first, we laugh at E – I mean, who wants to
put their mouth over that scrubby inflator to
try and blow it up? You'd catch every kind of
disease invented.

But E looks pleadingly at us, and V does it. 'I'm immune,' she says. She puts her lips to the valve and blows and blows.

We find a nearby mud slope and take turns sliding down it on the rubber ring. We have a good laugh. We ride on it all morning. V has to blow it back up every fifteen minutes, but she doesn't mind.

Then, we try and all ride on it at the same time. We spot a boy called C watching us by some trees. He takes a picture of us with his phone as we slide down the slope. We wave at him and the ring pops! We explode into the mud, sploshing through it in a heap of limbs. It's brilliant.

I am glad, because earlier, L had been really

fed up. She does not have V's wrestling skills, so she and E weren't able to even get anywhere near yesterday's box of donated shoes. The two of them are wearing sandals made from old tyres by the Sandal Man, who gives them away in exchange for bread. They're not very good. L's ankles are rubbed raw and E has a blister on his heel. Neither of them complain, but I can tell they are envious of V's trainers. The rubber ring ride takes all our minds off it.

Plus, I find *another* plastic figure! This one is a policeman.

We smell something cooking, and we follow the smell and find some people sitting around a fire, who have boiled up a big pot of soup. We stand and stare at them for ages. E goes right up to one of the people, and rubs his belly and shows off his best hungry look. They try and shoo him away but, eventually, they let us have a little soup each. This is turning into a good day.

Then the Guards come and put out the people's fire. They say the fire is made from burning plastic and is making toxic fumes that are bad for our health. This is silly. Being hungry is bad for our health. The Guards say everybody will have to move soon anyway, as there is going to be a clear-out.

V kicks ashes at the Guards' legs, which can't be good for the trainers. But the trainers are completely caked in mud anyway – already – so I suppose it doesn't make any difference. But V's mood is ruined. She is grumpy again, muttering under her breath. I don't think it's so bad. After all, the Guards didn't put out the fire until *after* we'd had our soup, did they?

I am playing with the plastic policeman, twizzling it around my fingers, listening to V swearing, and I have an idea.

'What's your favourite colour?' I ask L.

L thinks for a second. Then she says, 'Blue, like the sky.'

And then I ask E for his favourite colour. He scrunches his face up and thinks. Then he says, 'Blue, like the sky.'

I shake my head. 'Uh-uh. You can't have blue. You have to pick your own colour. Special to you.'

He grins. 'Red!' he calls. 'Like blood.'

'Don't you want to choose a nicer colour than that?' L asks him.

'Blood!' he insists. 'Blood!'

'Are you sure?'

E makes out like he's got a dagger in his hand. L rolls her eyes.

'Fair enough,' I say. 'V?'

V glances down at E, who still has the idea of blood dancing behind his eyes. Then she fixes her gaze on me. 'Black,' she says.

Black I think.

'Like night,' she adds, just to make sure I get the idea. 'Or death.' Everybody is really jolly today.

'Actually,' I say, 'black isn't really a colour. You need to choose a real colour.'

'All right,' she says, and she fixes her stubborn gaze on me. 'Brown,' she says.

'Brown,' I repeat. 'Yes, brown. Mud. Very funny.'

She shrugs. But says nothing.

'Blue, red, and brown,' I say then, after a pause.

Then I wait for one of them to ask me for my favourite colour. Nobody does. So in the end I say, 'Green. My favourite colour is green. Like grass. Open fields. Leaves.'

'Mould,' mutters V.

I look at her. 'Green,' I say. 'The colour of your eyes.' I smile at her.

L smiles at V too, and that makes E grin at her, from ear to ear. V folds her arms and looks down, studying the mud on her new trainers, ignoring us all.

I am ten now. Ten is a responsible age.

I take the plastic figure of the policeman, and the soldier and the gladiator and the doctor, and I go through the mud to the far side of the Camp where they are building the new youth club.

It rained this morning. Even though spring has slowly turned into summer, the rain keeps on coming. The muddy paths have come alive. Parts of the Camp are ankle deep in slush. After this, I'll need new trainers from Charity's shoebox myself.

The Camp is at its worst when it rains. Everything gets muddy – your food, your face, your bedding, your hair. The Camp has some shower blocks, but the water is cold and by the time you've walked back from the showers to your own shed you're covered in mud again. If brown really was V's favourite colour, she'd be as happy as a pig in mud, wouldn't she? But I know what she's really thinking of. She's thinking of white – a white bath, a white dressing gown, white slippers – of a new home in her auntie's posh village. A shiny white bath, shampoo and soap, bubbles, a soft white towel.

Not brown. Not this brown sludge everywhere.

The volunteers are busy with their hammers and nails and planks of wood and sheets of corrugated iron. The new youth club is almost finished. All it needs is the roof and some doors and furniture for the insides. Some of the men are painting the walls.

I have a word with the man in charge, called Adrian. He's a volunteer too, and he has hair that goes down to his shoulders, almost as long as Charity's. Ade is friendly. I tell him what I want, and why, and three times he nods his head and says, 'Not a problem.' But the fourth time, he frowns and puts his hand to his head to think about it.

'Give me twenty minutes,' he says. 'I'll see what I can do. Meanwhile, you wait here. If you help the boys painting the walls while you wait, we'll call it a fair exchange. Deal?'

'Deal,' I say, and we shake on it.

*

It's good to work, helping with the walls. One of the worst things about being stuck in the Camp is it's so boring. There is nothing to do but look for food, or for things to burn to keep warm. In the winter, anything that burns is used for fires. There is a school, but it is not a real school – it's just a holey tent with some planks of wood and writing slates. There's only room for a dozen pupils and everybody comes from different countries and speaks different languages and are all different ages, so lessons don't make much sense.

I went once or twice. Time would be better spent trying to hunt for food, but the Guards say we must all learn to write – not just our names, but our stories too, to recollect stories from our

Life Books. 'Tell us in words we understand,' they say. 'Speak to us in our language,' they say.

Painting the walls of the youth club is good work, and I see that there is blue paint, and red, and green. The volunteers and I finish painting the walls and Adrian still hasn't returned, so I reach into my pockets and I bring out the plastic figures. I take one of the figures and dangle it by the thread from Charity's blanket into a tin of blue paint. It is like fishing.

When I pull the figure out it is totally blue. I slide the top of the thread under a full tin of paint that's resting on the top of a table, and the blue figure dangles down from the edge to dry. This blue puppet is the puppet for L.

I then do the same with another plastic

figure, with some red paint, for E. Then I do the same with green paint. The figures spin as they hang from the tabletop, their colours shining in the daylight where the roof hasn't been fitted on.

The plastic figures are no longer a soldier, a gladiator and a doctor. In our own colours, they are now L and E and I. I look at them dangling, the fresh paint all bright and new. An L, an I, and an E. A real, true family, not in the past or the future, but here and now. Especially when V's puppet is added, wearing its new coat of paint. L and I and V and E.

I'm sitting on a mat, watching them dangle and dry, dangle and dry. The boy called C takes a picture of them as he passes by, like he always does. Adrian still hasn't come back. I'm beginning to wonder if I might have to let V have her grumpy-bum way, when in comes Ade looking very pleased with himself.

'Seems like it's your lucky day,' he says. He reaches into his pocket and brings out the smallest tin of paint I've ever seen. 'I had to beg a few favours to get this,' he says, 'but if it puts the sunshine back on that girl's face, it'll be worth it.'

I look at the tin. The final figure has a flat base under its feet, to keep it standing up, and the tin is so tiny I'm not sure the figure will fit through the hole for the lid.

Ade sees me puzzling over this. 'It's modelling paint, for model aeroplanes,' he explains. 'Do *not* ask me how I managed to get hold of it. This too.'

He hands me a brush, which is so small it's even shorter and thinner than a pencil. 'Paint away,' he says.

And I do. V pretends that her favourite colour is the colour of mud. My mum used to say there is beauty in everything. If the sun comes out, and you look out across the Camp at the sludge pits and puddles that turn everywhere into a swamp after days of rain, the mud isn't brown any more. Not in the sunlight.

The mud is gold.

So gold is the colour I paint the final puppet.

Gold, for V.

V, I, L, E

Today the mud is not gold. It's been raining. The mud is brown and sticky. While L and E are scratching round in the mud, hunting for treasure, V comes over to speak with me.

I can tell straight away that she's been up to something, because she has that sparky-eyed look on her face.

I'm sat leaning against the outside wall of the shack and she plonks herself next to me. The wall almost gives way against the two of us, but I say nothing because she gives me a cheeky grin.

'What's up?' I say.

'Guess what I got?' she says.

I don't know. 'A bazooka?' I say.

'Nope.'

'A monkey on a bicycle?'

'Nope.'

'A fridge full of footballs?'

'Nope.'

'Stilts?'

'Nope.'

'Rabies?'

'Not even close.'

'All right,' I say, 'I give up.'

'No, go on,' she says. 'Have one more guess.'

'I don't know. A treasure chest full of elephants.'

'Closer,' she says. 'Go on, one more try.'

'No. I'm bored now. And tired. What do you want, V?'

'Guess what I've got?'

'JUST TELL ME!'

She goes all wide-eyed and purses her lips as if she's surprised by my bad manners. She reaches for something in her pocket, but she leaves her hand there.

'It's . . .' She leans in close. 'A . . .' she whispers in my ear. 'Visa.'

What?

A visa really is a treasure chest. If you haven't got a Life Book, a visa is the next best thing.

It is another way of telling your story, but it is signed off and approved by the people in charge. *This story is a true story.* A visa is written in the language of the Guards and it can get you anywhere.

I can't believe V has managed to get herself a visa. If she has, she's out of here. She'll be tucked up in a comfy bed at her auntie's before you can say, 'Yespleasesorrythankyou.'

It's like all your birthdays come at once.

'I don't believe you,' I say to her.

'It's true.' She waggles her fingers inside her pocket. 'Do you want to see?'

'I do.'

She pulls her hand back out of her pocket, and I see straight away that it is true – V has got herself a visa. But it is the wrong type of visa. It is not a passport visa she has, it is a Visa *card*.

A Visa card is a piece of plastic with your name, and numbers, on it. And if the numbers are numbers that match up with your name, they will be read by a special reader inside a wall. If the reader likes your name, and the numbers match your name, it will give you cash. Loads and loads of cash.

I think about this. *Loads and loads of cash.* Enough cash to be able to buy a new Life Book.

And food.

And toys.

And new shoes.

And a home.

But a Visa doesn't give you enough cash to

allow you to smile for your picture in your Life Book, however much you are happy with your loads of cash. Even when you are rich, in your Life Book you must always remember to look sad. But who cares? Cash! A Life Book! Freedom to pass into a new home. Safe and friendly and warm.

In a way, Visa cards and visa papers are the same thing.

I am amazed.

'I stole it from a Guard,' V tells me.

I can't imagine how V managed to steal this from one of the Guards, but I do know you cannot go around stealing things. If it's not yours, it's not yours. I give her a look. She shrugs her shoulders.

I shake my head at her in disapproval. I inspect the Visa card.

There might be masses of money on this card, thousands and thousands. But in an instant I realise V will never lay her hands on any of it. My heart sinks.

'V,' I say, 'this is no use to you. It has the Guard's name on it. Not yours. This won't fool anybody. It's a man's name, and you are a girl.'

V stares at the card for a long time.

Finally, she says, 'You are a man.' She looks at me hopefully.

V makes me feel sad.

'I am a boy,' I say. 'A little boy.'

'Hmph,' she says.

For a few moments, we sit in silence. I wish V had actually got herself a real visa. Imagine, an actual bunch of papers, written by a responsible adult, telling V's story: her name and the names of all her family and where she was born, and what her family did for a living and who were her sisters and brothers, and where she went to school and had her holidays, and her uncles and aunties and where they lived and what they did, and where V was allowed to travel to, anywhere in the whole world, signed off and dated at the bottom of the story with the author's name. It'd be fantastic.

I wish I had one. I wish we all had one.

She looks down at the piece of plastic in her hand.

'I could sell it to Ade,' she says. 'And use the money to buy a new Life Book.'

I don't even tell her that Ade doesn't deal in stolen goods. He's one of Charity's lot.

'Good luck with that,' I say to her. I get up to go and join the others scratching in the mud.

A little while later, Ade arrives to give E one of his regular schoolings. L is worried that her brother isn't learning how to read and write, and will never be able to share his story. Ade has offered to help.

Ade is teaching E to read and write using a stick in the mud. He asks E to spell a word, and if E spells it wrongly, he takes the stick and spells it the right way. Then he gives the stick

back to E, who must copy the correct spelling.
It is pretty basic.

I watch them.

'Spell "school",' says Ade.

E takes the stick and scratches in the mud.

SCOOL

'Pretty good,' says Ade. He takes the stick
and makes the correct spelling. E copies it.

'Excellent. Spell "write", as in "writing
something down".'

E scratches in the mud.

RITE

E isn't the best speller in the world.

'You're getting much better,' Ade praises him. 'Just add a W – see?'

WRITE

V comes up and stands next to me, watching with a grumpy look on her face.

'Okay,' says Ade, 'now try "read".'

E takes the stick.

RAED

'Very good! Almost perfect.'

V sniggers. I nudge her in the ribs. Just because she's in a mood because her Visa is useless, doesn't mean she should take it out on E.

Ade spells the word correctly and gives the stick back to E. E grips it determinedly, and scratches.

R A E D

Again.

'You're making a really good effort,' says Ade.

'Huh!' V butts in. 'No wonder nobody ever believes the stories we tell. Look at us: uneducated, unlearned, and ... and.' She snatches the stick from E. 'This is what we are,' she says. 'And all that we'll ever be.'

She scratches in the mud so angrily the stick

snaps in two. She finishes her writing with the stub gripped in her fist, like a dagger.

She steps away from her work and throws the dagger to the ground, before stomping off in a huff.

Ade, E and I look down at what she's spelled.

U N R A E D

This is what we are. And all that we'll ever be.

I pick up what's left of the stick and scratch over the top of the words, until there's nothing left but scrawl.

The sun is shining and the mud is drying into hard ruts.

I am going to *do* something. Something we can celebrate. Something to make up for our missing Life Books, the lies, V's scratches in the mud.

This morning, I unlock the padlock on our shed door and sneak out before L and E are awake. The padlock is a bit of a joke really. Our shack is loosely hammered together from bits of chipboard and tarpaulin. We have a window made of see-through corrugated plastic, glued on. If the big bad wolf came and huffed and puffed he could easily blow our house down.

I am going to find some food for E. He hasn't eaten properly for days. Some proper food. I have a box of matches which I have been saving for when they'll come in most useful.

I'm heading for Deep Ditch. I have a scarf to cover my mouth because the smell is bad. But it is the rubbish and decay that is actually the attraction. Although it is not an attraction to *me*. Ade gave me a tip. A tip about a tip. It is not just me and the others camped here who have been on the move. Birds travel from country to country too. And some birds, big birds that use up a lot of energy flapping their big wings – they decide it is better for them to travel less, and eat more.

Big birds, like storks. When I gazed up at the sky last night, I saw one. Actually, I saw two. Then I saw three. Their wings like paper kites above our heads. I thought of the stories my mum used to tell me about the storks delivering new babies. I pictured the circling storks bringing one baby after another to the Camp, dropping them from their giant beaks at Charity's feet, for her to mother.

But I am ten now. I have too many responsibilities to be thinking such nonsense. The storks are not circling around the Camp bringing us babies. They are here for the food. Storks don't worry about the smell or the decay. There is nothing they like more than pecking through the rubbish tip, looking for some rotten food or other.

Big birds, storks.

I have my knife, the one I use for shaping my puppet sticks. And I am big now, bigger than I used to be. And hungry.

Imagine the faces on L and E when I return to our shack with the best breakfast we've had in months.

And V's face when I tell her the story of my hunt. It'll be a story she can write down, like in a proper book for people to actually *read*.

Storks have long legs, for wading through mud. And I know what that means, from trudging around the Camp. If you are up to your knees in it, you can't just leap away in a shot. All I have to do is sneak up on one till I'm close enough to pounce. From behind. Stab my knife through the back of its neck, down into its heart.

Deep Ditch is rank today. The summer sun is making it stink. People throw food bones here, which is what brings the storks. People empty their toilets here too. Blankets that have been burnt in the fires that break out around the Camp. Bandages. Busted chairs. Life jackets. Shoes rotted by marching from far away to here. Burger cartons brought in by people trying to help. Even through the scarf, the smell seeps in. It is *vile*.

I see my stork, picking through the worst of it, like treasure. I tighten the grip on my knife. The stork and I are not so different to each other. Looking for breakfast in the waste. Looking for food, any food.

I sneak behind it, as planned. The scarf is covering my mouth but the smell still makes me want to throw up. My feet are sinking as well, slowing my own moves.

I hadn't thought of that. Also, the stork is a lot bigger up close. With its beak held high, it towers over me. And with its wings spread against the mist, its reach is way beyond that of my own arms, no matter how I might stretch them out like a monster. The stork can fly across oceans, it can spear fish with its deadly beak.

But I have my knife.

The stork I am stalking is picking at something scrunched into the sludge. A nappy. The bird is not very fussy. I try not to think about it. Stork meat will be like chicken, or turkey. Maybe. While I build the fire on which we will cook it, L and E will go and find V and give her the good news. Then they will call at the bus and we will invite Charity to eat with us too. Or, if she cannot come, we will save her some wing. I can taste it already.

I pounce.

I hear the sound of rifles. *Clitter-clat.* I freeze. I thought we were safe here in the Camp, miles from the soldiers.

Then I glimpse a flapping up above. It is the stork's mate, clattering its bill, a warning signal. Not guns.

My stork twists its neck around. Its black-raisin eye glints at me. At the same time, the beak swings like a sword and I stumble back in the mud. The beak opens and jerks forward.

Snippety-snap.

The stork stabs at my face. I swing at it, knocking its beak, but it tears away, my scarf in its beak. Then it spits the scarf out and snaps for my fingers. *Snip-snap*, like a pair of shears. I catch my breath. *Snip-snap*, at my chest.

Perhaps it is the *stork* who is thinking of *me* as breakfast.

I thrust my knife forward. The tip *clangs* against the bird's bill, like a swordfight. For a moment, we *fence* with each other. We dance together, a *click, clack, clang* of a dance.

Then the bird also stumbles in the mud, flapping its wings in a fury.

I feel the wind of it in my face.

I drop the knife.

The stork lunges.

I leap forward to meet it, my fingers grabbing blindly.

'Aaaargh!' I yell. It *clitter-clats* back at me.

I land face first in the mud. I roll over. The shape of it rises above me, into the sky, its whoosh of wings flapping its sure escape from me.

In my chest, my heart goes *boom boom boom* like distant bombs.

I breathe. The smell of waste and decay.

And, in my hand, the most perfect white feather I have ever seen.

I am covered from head to toe in brown, and I have to fish for my knife in the sludge. But in my other hand, the feather sits as white as fresh snow.

I think of E. He will wake hungry, and there will be nothing to take away his hunger. I have the feather. E will be sad. L will make fun, try to get him to laugh. I will have no food to offer.

I sit in the stink, and I am sad. The sun has risen from over the hill, yellow against the blue morning. I look at the feather, white. My ears hear the echo of the rifle-fire clatter of the stork.

Summer is all around. How can it be that I am trapped in a world of brown?

I look at the feather. At the blue sky.

Snippety-snap echoes in my ears. I raise my eyes and see the stork soaring away through the blue sky, gliding towards the far horizon.

If we had wings, we could fly to a faraway

land as well, instead of trudging back and forwards through our field of mud.

But we are stuck in the mud. We are here, whether the Guards believe our stories or not.

I see a gap in the fence. I stand, and wipe the sludge from my bottom. The feather, I hold away from the stains. I see the gap in the fence and I walk through it, away from Deep Ditch, thinking of E. Thinking of food. Wishing. Gripping the feather, squinting into the sun, I walk, through the grass, as far away from our shed as I like.

We are not actually locked inside the Camp. We're free to go whenever we wish.

Free to go *back*.

We might not actually be locked up, but we're blocked from going further *forward*. The Guards are here to stop us getting on any trains, to stop us from hitching a ride on a lorry, to stop us from getting on a boat, to stop us from walking into the tunnel that takes us to a place where there is plenty of food, and shelter, and warmth.

We are free to go *back*. To keep walking down past Deep Ditch, where the Camp opens out into the countryside, and the road back. The road home. But there is nothing to go back to. Our homes have been disappeared by bombs. Our families have been shot by soldiers. Our schools have been burnt.

Or we can just stay here. In the mud. It is

a free world. But even here nobody likes us, because the mud is too close to the homes and schools and shops that belong to the Guards and their families. If the Guards make sure we don't come any closer to the homes and the schools and the shops, then we are welcome to stay here, in our tents and wooden huts.

No further forwards.

If they ignore us long enough maybe they think we'll just simply disappear into the mud.

The further from the Camp I walk, the more the colour of summer sparkles. Green, the colour I chose for my puppet, bright and light in the newness of leaves; poppies; red berries, ripe for picking, a feast for the day.

Berries.

I walk up to a brambly bush, squint at the red fruit. I remove my shirt, tie a knot in the bottom, and reach out my hand. I pop a berry through the hole for my neck. The berry drops down to the knot I tied at the bottom, and I remember. So long ago, when we had streets and shops and tables and meals. Once, Mum took me and my sisters to a sweet shop and there were a hundred different types of sweet, and we took a bag each and we picked a sweet and popped it into the bag. And then another, and then another.

This is what I do now, with the berries! I pick myself a shirt full. For every one I drop into my T-shirt bag, I pop one into my mouth, the lushness trickling across my tongue.

The white feather is tucked behind my ear. The sun warms the back of my neck. I snap a little branch of large bright green leaves from a tree and waft it back and forth like a fan, cooling my face. I feel wild and free.

I could just keep walking, away from the Camp. I could go and find a new life. But I have no family. I do not even have an auntie, in a warm house in a pretty village, to try and dodge past the Guards and get to. There is nothing for me to do but wander back to the Camp.

'Who wants a feast?' I say, as I arrive at our hut.

L and E are lying on the ground, legs and arms sprawled out, still and stiff.

A little further away, another shack is burning. Two Guards guard it while it crackles and crumples.

My friends, on their backs. Flies buzz and bother about their heads, but they do not move.

'Hello?' I say.

Well, I'm sure they haven't died of starvation while I was away, as hungry as we all are. Have they?

'Hey!' I say. Smoke drifts across the beams of sunlight in front of our hut.

They wouldn't be poisoned. You can't be poisoned, because to get poisoned you have to actually eat something first. But they do not move. Have they been attacked? That is just as unlikely. Who's going to attack a couple of skinny kids?

I step right up to them. They have their eyes closed, dead to the world.

'Hey!' I repeat. 'Who wants a feast?'

'Shsh,' says a voice above my ear.

I turn round and look up. V.

'Rarrrrrgh!' L and E leap up and charge at me.

'Sleeping Lions,' V explains. 'Leaping Lions. You lose.'

'Rarrrrgh!' L dances around me, pretending to claw at me. E has wrapped his arms around my leg and clamped his mouth over my kneecap, gnawing softly at the bone. It is tickly and soggy through the rip in my jeans. I try and shake him off, but he tightens his grip. 'Mmph, mmph,' he goes. 'Mmph, mmph.' He is sucking me to death.

'I am the Queen of the Jungle!' V declares, going for my shoulder. Then she sees I have something bundled up in my shirt.

'What you got?' she says, snatching at the shirt.

'Careful!' I shriek, but I'm smiling. She thrusts her hand down through the neck and brings back a fistful of red. Her eyes almost pop out with delight and she gives me an ear-to-ear grin.

Then her eyes dart down to L and E, still trying to maul me to the ground. 'Here, kitty-kats,' she says, opening her palm. 'Fresh blood and guts.'

Their fingers dig into the pile of berries in an instant. I don't mind. It's a great sackful. We have ourselves a feast.

'Who wants to play?' I say. With bellies full, now is the perfect time to bring out my family of puppets.

I found some fresh, straight twigs, and whittled them with a dinner knife to make them even smoother. The paint dried splendidly on each of the figures. L, E and V all have big smiles on their faces when they see the puppets painted in their favourite colour.

I can tell that V is (not so) secretly pleased that I've made her puppet shiny gold instead of dull brown. I was worried that V might think herself too grown-up to be mucking around with puppets. But she practically snatches it out of my hand, and almost forgets to say thank you before jiggling it up and down. You're never too old to play.

'I'm going to kick that Guard's ass,' she makes the puppet say. 'Then I'm going to catch a train and live in a proper house. Then I shall enter a talent show and be famous forever.'

E takes hold of his red puppet, and he *does* forget to say thank you before making his red man run after V's golden girl, saying, 'I'll be your bodyguard, and keep you safe from all your fans. You'll always need me by your side!'

L takes the blue puppet and she walks it up to the green puppet, which is mine. Her puppet says to my puppet, 'Would you like to dance?'

We dance across fields full of flowers.

It's only pretend, of course. We're still in the Camp, in the drizzle and mud. The mud is so runny it's flowing between the fences. It sucks because if you look through the fences outside the Camp, summer is here and there really are bright green leaves on the trees.

I stop looking. Around us, V's golden puppet sparkles and shines as she travels from one holiday to the next, the red puppet always two steps behind her, beating off autograph hunters and fans.

We spend the whole morning creating stories for our puppet people. Adventures and romances that haven't yet happened to us. Not lies though, just pretend.

And it is during our puppet play that we discover O.

O is shy at first, watching us from behind what's left of a burnt-out shed. He thinks we can't see him, but L spots him and gives me a little look and a tilt of her head. So I look, and I see O too. Then V sees him, and E too.

We carry on playing and, slowly, O comes nearer. He is covered in mud from head to toe. He looks as though he has climbed out of Deep Ditch, where I rolled around in the mud fighting the stork. I was covered head to toe as well, and so was the stork. O is a mud baby.

O's round eyes shine through. It is the same

when he smiles, a flash of teeth sparkling out through the brown. He looks like one of the puppets that's been painted head to toe – but with mud.

After a while, he is only a few feet away, transfixed by the puppets. V has been watching him, and she turns her golden puppet to face O, and jerks the thread so the puppet gives a little skip. 'Hello,' she says, in the puppet's voice. 'Isn't it a lovely day? What's your name, little boy?'

V smiles. It's the second time in one day that V has smiled. Twice in one day is a record for V.

The little boy says, 'O.'

'Hello, O,' says V in her own voice. 'Would you like to play with us?'

L, O, V, E

Now we pretend that our puppets have bellies stuffed full of berries, so full that they can hardly walk, and we make them slump along in a big line – my green puppet, L's blue puppet, E's red puppet, and V's golden one. I had to restring V's puppet because it snapped. It's okay, because I have a collection of thread. I don't tell Charity I collect stray threads from her blanket because she might think it bad manners.

O doesn't have a puppet, and in any case

hasn't told us what is his favourite colour. If he cannot even tell us his favourite colour, how can he tell the Guards anything at all, about who he is, where his family is, and where he is from? If O doesn't speak, how can he ever have his story written down? How will he be able to pass through the ports? He will be here forever, until he is an old man.

O sits on an upturned bucket, chin on his fists. But L and I, and V and E, turn our puppets towards him and make them dance.

O smiles up at us, and his hands dangle down over his knees. He is like a little puppet himself, without any strings. He lifts one foot from the ground. He raises an arm, bent and limp-wristed. He crooks his head to the side, in a question. E giggles. V laughs out loud. And L dangles her puppet in front of his face. Her puppet asks, 'Do you want to dance?'

Yes, he wants to dance. He lifts up his other hand, raises his other knee, and wobbles forward.

For a moment, he reminds me of the stork – how it almost tore the skin from my cheek. But I put the thought out of my mind. We might not have had roasted stork, but we had berries – so many that I was even able to hold a few back for later. And in any case, O is not a stork, he is just a toddler. He pretends to have no strength in his arms, and L has hold of one wrist, and V the other. The two of them make his arms dance like they are pulling his strings.

'La la,' he sings. 'La la.'

I tickle him beneath the chin with the tip of my white feather, and it makes him giggle as he sings.

All of us dance and the sun shines on the mud like a mother's smile.

O plays with us for the rest of the afternoon. When we go in search of food, he tags along.

'Where's his mum?' L says to me, as we trudge our way through a particularly sticky mud pit. 'Where's his mum?'

I look at her. I think she is thinking of her own mum. Hers and E's. Where is *their* mum?

The sludge goes up almost to my knees. V has got her trainers off and is holding them up, so they do not get totally destroyed. Mine are already more mud than leather, so I don't bother. Sometimes, having sandals like L and E is the best thing, when you live in a world of mud.

V is also carrying O, on her shoulders.

O is carrying our puppets, two in each fist, dangling down in front of V's face.

When L asks where is O's mum, she means *is he an unaccompanied minor?* But O can't be an unaccompanied minor. O can't be more than three. And the only word he seems to know is 'O'. Surely he has somebody looking out for him?

We are heading towards the children's bus because Charity sometimes has spare biscuits, if it's been a good day and visitors have brought gifts. Sometimes we get crisps, and fizzy drinks.

This week has been full of bad days. Twice, we ate nothing all day. We shared some water. Today, we have only eaten berries. So we really *really* hope that Charity has some crisps and fizzy drinks.

As we make our way towards the bus, O is humming a tune from the tower-top of V's head. It doesn't have any words, just 'La la, la la, la la.' His fingers are bouncing the puppets up and down in front of him, so it seems as if they are dancing to the 'La la, la la.'

V gave him her jumper because he was only wearing raggedy old clothes and was shivering in the drizzle. The jumper is too big for him, so it looks cosy and warm. I think O has decided that we are a good gang to join.

At the bus, Charity greets us with a box of crackers. But there's no cheese or anything to put on them, and between the five of us the crackers last for about thirty seconds. Eating a handful of crackers makes me feel even hungrier.

Charity has a whole heap of kids who sleep on her bus at night, and most of them are here now. I think that's why there isn't any food, because she's already fed so many. There are nineteen of them: K, X, S, A, F, P, G, Y, J, W, M, D, N, B, Q, R, H, T, and Z. They are all pestering her, hoping she'll pull out a hidden bar of chocolate. But there is no food left, and Charity has to shoo them away in order to speak to us.

O climbs up onto Charity's knee. 'Hello, little one,' says Charity. O gazes dreamily up at Charity's face.

'Who is he?' asks L. 'Where's his mum?'

'He's called O,' says Charity. But we already know that. Charity shrugs. 'I don't know who his mother is. Or where she might be.'

'Do you have a Life Book?' V asks O. 'Any papers?'

'O,' says O.

It's a good question. Even little babies have to have a Life Book, even when they're so young they don't yet have a story to tell. The Life Book will tell the story of the baby's mum and dad. It will say when the baby was born, and where it was born. It will have a picture of the baby's face. It is only babies who are allowed to smile in their Life Book picture, but they are not allowed to hold a toy.

'Where's your mummy?' asks L, again. 'Where's your daddy?'

'O,' says O, and jiggles up and down in Charity's lap.

'He's been staying on the bus,' says Charity. 'I found him a few days ago, wandering around on his own.'

'Do you think his mum is in the Camp?' I ask. 'He might have got lost.'

'I've been asking,' says Charity. 'But quietly.'

'Quietly?'

Charity tickles the end of O's nose. 'I don't want to hand him over to just anyone.'

Just anyone. Not everyone in the Camp is as friendly as V and I, or L and E.

'The problem is,' Charity continues, 'I can't keep watch on him all the time. He keeps wandering off.'

'La la, la la,' O sings. 'La la, la la.' He rests his head against Charity's chest and smiles up at her.

E looks up, resting his own head against the side of Charity's leg. 'La la,' he sings, under his breath.

L strokes E's head but she can't take her eyes from O. 'What about the Guards?' says L. 'Shouldn't they be taking care of O?'

Charity shakes her head. 'No passport.' She frowns. 'No story. O doesn't exist. He's not their problem.'

'He's not anybody's *problem*,' snaps V. 'He's just a toddler. Barely more than a baby.'

'He does exist,' I add. 'He's here. Right now.'

The boy C appears from out of nowhere, like he always does. As he climbs onto the bus he winks at us.

He hugs Charity and she beams at him. Her hand strokes the back of his neck.

'Got your phone?' Charity asks him.

'Course I have,' says C. 'What am I, a muppet?'

E giggles and says, 'Muppet!'

L waggles her arms at him, like she's a muppet too. Like we're all muppets.

C is not a muppet. He is Charity's son. He is really old, almost seventeen. Charity tells us that C's school is on holiday, which is why he's here.

'Some holiday camp,' says C. And he points his phone at me, and says, 'Gotcha.'

I don't know what he wants *my* picture for. I bet I look a proper mess.

And *C*'s not his real name either. He just calls himself that so he can fit in, be the same as the rest of us, rather than just a visitor,

He *is* a visitor though, isn't he? Charity catches his eyes, and then she looks at O.

'Hey,' says C, 'O?'

O looks at C. C taps his phone. He looks at the screen. 'Niiice. Hey, O, who's the superstar?'

I don't know if O understands a word C says, but he toddles forwards and looks at the screen. On the screen it is him. He smiles. 'O!'

Charity nods at C, and C nods back at her, like they've settled something.

'Things to do,' says C, 'places to go.' He kisses his mum and he wanders off.

'Kids,' says Charity, rolling her eyes.

I try and remember, when was the final time I kissed my mum. It is difficult to remember.

'I'm hungry,' says E.

'You're boring,' says V.

See? E's always hungry. That's the story of his life, and it is never going to change.

'You're ugly,' E shoots back at her.

'You're smaller than me,' V says, cracking her knuckles.

'There's no need to bicker,' says Charity. 'Go

down to the south-east corner of the Camp, just past the smashed-up showers. Word is, someone's got a big cook-in going on there. There's a meeting. You might be lucky.'

'What about O?' says V.

'He's hungry too,' Charity answers. 'But bring him back before dark. I want him back on the bus, safe and sound.'

It's only after we set off, L and V swinging O between them, that I realise Charity must be hungry too. She didn't even eat any of the crackers.

But I know what she would say. She would say what she always says.

'Don't worry about me. I have a home. I can go home anytime I wish.'

Charity has a Life Book. Nobody is accusing her of making up lies.

By the time we reach the cook-in, there is nothing left. Everybody is busy talking about the Guards threatening to close down part of the Camp. People barely notice us. But one man gives O a tub of yoghurt.

E looks on, trying his hardest to contain himself. He knows that if he was the youngest, it's him would have been given the yoghurt. But he's not youngest any more is he? He gets to lick the lid, and scrape his finger around the empty pot. He looks up at L, because she hasn't even licked the lid, and she is his sister.

'It's all right,' L says to him. 'I'll find something later.'

V and I say nothing. It is an unwritten rule: the youngest gets first pick of any food. No 'ifs' or 'buts'.

O has wrapped his arms around V's leg.

I gaze up at the sky, the vast blue expanse above us. All the space in the world. But no storks. Not today.

'We've got to get out of this place,' says L.

'Oi, C!' V shouts.

C is sitting under a tree, fiddling with his phone. He's been taking our picture – again. He looks up as V calls out his name.

'Show us your Life Book,' says V.

I am shocked by her bad manners.

C glances at us, in suspicion. 'Why?' he asks. Life Books are like gold dust in the Camp.

V gives a shrug. 'I just wanted to look,' she says. 'I wondered, did your mum really name you Child C? Because if she did, it was a bit cruel, don't you think?'

My jaw drops open. V is so rude!

But C smiles at us. 'If you knew what she actually called me, you'd know how cruel my mum really is. Anyway,' he goes on, 'I reckon that if none of you kids who live in the Camp are allowed to use your full names, then I shouldn't either.'

'Solidarity,' says V, sarcastically.

'It's not C's fault,' I mutter at her, 'that we're all trapped in the Camp.'

'While he's free to come and go, just as he pleases?'

'Exactly,' I say. 'And he's here, isn't he, when he could be back at home playing with his mates.'

But I wonder, maybe he just wants to stay close to his mum. Who can blame him? He's an *accompanied minor*. I'd cling close to my mum, if she was here.

A serious look comes over C's face, and he stands up and walks towards us.

'Seymour,' he says. 'Child C, it is short for Seymour. Not exactly the coolest name in the world, is it?'

V and I don't know what to say to that.

'It is funny though,' C goes on, 'don't you think?'

'Funny?' I ask.

C points his phone at us, and takes another picture.

'Seymour,' he says. 'Don't you get it? *See. More.* Seymour, yes?'

He chuckles to himself, like this is one of the funniest things ever. V and I just look at each other, as if he is a bit weird.

'Well, Seymour,' says V. 'Maybe you can point us towards a place where we can *see more* food?'

V has the worst manners of any kid in the whole of the Camp.

We wander back to the shack and see Ade standing outside it, with E. I wonder if he's having another go at teaching E to spell. He catches sight of us and I bet he's worried that V is going to trash the class again.

But Ade isn't teaching E. He is being extra-smiley. And he is trying to learn something *from* him.

'You're one of the best pupils I ever had,' he tells E.

E smiles back at Ade.

'So tell me, E,' Ade says to him, nice and soft. 'What's your name, really? Apart from E, I mean. What were you called in the time before you came to the Camp? I bet you have a fabulous name. I bet it's much better than a silly name like *Adrian*. Would you tell me?'

E frowns, as if he is thinking about it. He

looks down at the ground. Like he is trying to remember.

'Well?' says Ade.

But E carries on looking at the ground.

'Maybe it was Ejaz?' says Ade. 'Or Elyas?'

E does not respond.

Ade knows that E doesn't have any papers, no Life Book, no nothing. He's been trying to find out E's name for ages.

'Ezatullah?'

When E still doesn't answer, Ade winks, and says, 'Elvis?'

L has wandered over with O.

E stares at Ade, and he takes O's hand.

'He *does* know his real name,' L says to Ade. She sounds apologetic. 'Just tell him,' she says to E.

'E,' says E.

'O,' says O.

E points at something, and he and O toddle away.

'I'm sorry,' L says to Ade.

'It's all right,' Ade answers. 'Sometimes it's better to leave the past in the past.'

Not when the present is like this, I think. But I say nothing. The Guards want us to tell them our life stories in *their* language, but our names are our names, whatever language you speak or spell.

E might well remember his name from before. Maybe he remembers exactly what happened to him. Maybe that is all best left behind. Don't let the past come back. He is just Child E now.

He doesn't have a real name any more. None of us do.

I am tired. I go and find a tree to sleep under.

Sometimes I go to sleep hungry, and sometimes I go to sleep not so hungry. But mostly I go to sleep hungry.

Then, when I sleep, I dream of not being hungry. I dream of chocolate cake, of fresh-baked bread, of olives and lemons and oranges and of roast chicken, at parties and picnics, surrounded by my mother and father, my sisters and brothers, and aunties and uncles, laughing and joking, our bellies full.

Today, as I doze under the tree, my belly full of berries, I dream of Life Books. I dream of L and O and V and E, and the words we need to set us free.

And I dream of the stork, of how I am less than a little boy, how I am a tiny baby. In my dream I am in a basket hanging by a ribbon hooked onto the beak of the stork. The stork is beating its wings silently, flying high through the sky, away from the warning *clitter-clat* of the rifles, over the barbed wire, to a new land, a new home, to family and friends and fun, and life.

And in the basket, in my wrinkled old-man baby hands, I grip the white feather from the stork's beating wings. And in my baby fingers I twizzle the feather until it sits like a pen. I hold the feather pen up to the whiteness of the sky, and up against the billowing clouds, I begin to write.

My name.

I wake to the shouts of men in the Camp, arguing with the Guards.

The Guards are pushing the men and threatening to hit them with their clubs. The men are shouting at the Guards, pointing their fingers at them and slicing at the air in anger. It is like this every day. But every day people become more and more angry. Every day, somebody is struck by the Guards and has to be helped away, their head bleeding.

Today, there are more Guards, a larger crowd, louder shouting.

My dream is broken, but I do not forget it.

The crowd is angry, because a bulldozer is making its way along the path, snorting like a dragon. Its wheels send mud splattering against the washing that people have hung up to dry in the sun. Its great digger catches on the corners of shacks and knocks them wonky. It hooks itself onto wooden chairs and snaps them into pieces. The crowd race behind it, shouting and shaking their fists.

As the bulldozer trundles through the Camp, I think of my dream, of writing my name with the feather I won from the stork. I remember the stash of red berries I set aside for when hunger comes back to me. I pick up the branch of leaves I'd cast on the floor outside the door when I returned to our shack.

I step back into our shack, into the corner where I have my box of stuff, and grab the bunch of Charity's thread I laid carefully in an empty rice packet.

Outside, the sound of the bulldozer churning up mud, lifting the smell of old poo and rot, wafting it across our space. I step out, and fan the air in front of me with my leaves, to get rid of the smell. I make my way to the quiet spot at the very edge of the Camp. I know what to do.

My task requires a steady hand and a keen eye, but I have both. I painted the puppets. I used to paint pictures, which my mum stuck on the fridge door, back when . . .

I carefully pluck the biggest leaf from my branch of leaves.

I pick the biggest berry from my stash, fat with juice.

I poke the berry with the tip of the feather. Red squirts out and hits me in the eye. I jab the point back in, and I twizzle. Then I pull the feather out, and the juice drips onto my knee. Quickly, I put the point of the feather to the surface of a leaf. It makes a red blotch, and when I scratch at it, the blotch smears. Now, the tip of the feather is dry.

Once, at school, we watched a film with ancient scholars in it. Or actors, I suppose. It all looked a lot easier when the actor wrote with a feather, in the film, a thousand years in the past.

None of the children in the Camp celebrate their birthday. None of us even get a birthday card. None of us have a Life Book.

I will use the quill and the berry juice and the leaves to make Life Books for us all.

I am hungry again, and thirsty, by the time I hurry back to the Camp. The bird song seems less jolly behind me, the closer I get to the bad-tempered sounds of this place I cannot call home.

Today, it is full with puffs of smoke, the smell of burning rubber.

So I make an effort. I tell myself to remember.

I fill my mind with the memory of word games we used to play, from before.

I see my friends, V, L, E, and O. They are with Charity's son, C, from the children's centre. They are all in a ring, holding hands, dancing around in a circle.

'La la,' O is singing, 'la la.'

E is waggling his bottom. L is ducking her head up and down, up and down, like some kind of funny animal. Even V is singing 'La la, la la' too. As I get closer, I realise they are all singing O's song. But they are singing 'La la, la la' at different times to each other, and in different keys. And C is singing too, as out of tune as the rest of them. To be honest, it's a proper racket. But it drowns out the sounds of bad temper echoing from the rest of the Camp. Everybody is smiling.

C catches my eye as I dance towards them. I bring good news. I bring further games. I nod at C.

'Hey,' I say, 'what's happening?'

'We're playing O's *La la* game,' C answers, separating himself from the dancing ring. 'Yourself?'

I smile a lopsided smile. 'I was going to ask who wants to play,' I say. 'But everybody's already playing.'

'What have you got?' says C.

'A play tree,' I say. 'Just on the other side of Deep Ditch.'

'In the meadow?'

'Yes, over there.' I point.

He beams at me. 'La la la! That's exactly where we were going to take our dance.' He points his phone at the others, and I see he gets a picture. 'Come on, kids,' he calls. 'I's got a surprise!'

'Wait,' I yell. 'Everybody needs their puppets.'

L's blue puppet, E's red puppet, V's golden puppet, and my green one dance through the long grass. C and O dance together, C pretending to tug on O's strings. O is his own dancing puppet.

The air is full of pollen, of floating blowballs, greenflies and bees, all dancing a dance of their own around us to the music of the larks and tits and sparrows flitting through the hedges and bushes and trees.

I see my Play Tree at the bottom of the meadow, and lead the dance towards it. Everybody is having so much fun parading they do not notice, and it is only when we are really close up that V stops singing. She stops dancing too. She looks at me grinning. Her cheeks go red and she lets out a laugh.

Everybody stops.

In front of us, a long branch stretches into the sunlight of the meadow. The branch is full of green leaves.

The tree has other leaves too, that have not sprouted from buds on twigs, but dangle, rotating from thread strung to the tree, swaying in the breeze. Green leaves, with red letters.

There is a leaf for L.

There is a leaf for E.

There is a leaf for V.

There is a leaf for O.

And a leaf for me, I.

The dance of the puppets comes to a halt. Everyone looks up at their leaves, dancing their own dance, dangling from the branch in the breeze.

'I am making leaves for all the other children too,' I say.

The leaves rustle against each other.

'A Leaf Book,' says E.

'A Life Book,' says V.

'They are lovely,' says L.

'I thought,' I say, 'we could use them for games. Like you use cards, in a pack. I thought, maybe, we could use them for guess the word, missing letter, err … things like that. Maybe help us with our spelling.'

Suddenly I feel embarrassed. I look down at my feet. Maybe it's a stupid idea. After all, they are only leaves. They'll probably just rot, or drop off when it rains.

'It's a great idea,' says L.

And V says, 'Who wants to play?'

V, E, I, L.

For covering things.

V, O, L, E.

'Unh?' says E.

'It's a little furry creature,' says L. 'Like a mouse.'

O, L, I, V, E

To eat on a picnic.

'I used to love olives,' says V.

E, L, V, O, I.

'That's not a word,' says L.

'It is too,' says E.

We all stare at him.

'Elvoi,' he says. 'It means the feeling you get in your mouth when you open a bag of crisps.'

'Does it really?' says L.

'Yes,' E lies.

While everybody was playing with the leaves, I was looking at all the leaves on all the different trees and I was thinking that a leaf is like a heart that has been rolled over and around, over and around, for a long time. A tattered heart: ♥. I was pleased with myself. I was happy. I felt a little like I was at home.

O begins to sing his song. 'La la,' he chirrups. 'La la.'

Look at us, I think, *laughing and playing, a family of friends all together.*

How perfect life can be.

But then I hear the *clatter* of rifles. Echoing down the meadow from the Camp. I look up and

I see smoke. It's not the storks. It really *is* rifles. I hear the warning *clatter* again. Shouting. And a sound we haven't heard in the Camp, a sound none of us have heard since the day we had to grab what we could carry in our hands and flee from our homes: the sound of screaming.

'O,' says O.

The berries scatter across the grass as we leap up.

C snatches O up in his arms. 'O!' says O, stretching his hands towards the fallen fruit. 'O! O!'

But the screams and the shouts and the *clatter* are far louder.

All of us run, together, back to the Camp.

E, V, I, L

Plumes of smoke rise over the crest of the hill, as if the Camp is enjoying a dozen giant cook-ins.

We slip through the fence at Deep Ditch and the first thing we see is the bulldozers. Their engines are roaring, and the big diggers with sharpened teeth are clawing at the air. The air is thick with smoke. The mud is being turned up and into the air. It is everywhere. *Everywhere.* I start to splutter and choke.

V has raced ahead, faster than us. She turns

round to look at us and I see she is crying. I have known V go for three days without food and manage not to cry. She didn't cry when the Guard stole her shoes. She didn't cry when another Guard took her phone and ground it under his boot so she couldn't call her auntie. She did not even cry when a lorry driver found her smuggled in the back of his truck and he threw her onto the side of the road and she grazed her arm from shoulder to elbow. But she is crying now.

My own eyes start to sting and tear-up.

'Tear gas,' says C. Even as he speaks, I see he is taking a picture of the scene with his phone. He nudges me aside and grabs O roughly by the arm. 'This way.'

Through the clouds of tear gas I can see families from the Camp. Mothers running with their children, trying to protect their faces from the gas. I see Guards, bellowing. And men, throwing stones.

L stumbles in the mud, and I grab her arm, pull her up. 'What is happening?' I ask. 'What is happening?'

'This wasn't supposed to happen for another week,' yells V, as we catch up with her. 'We were told we were safe, for now.'

A burning barricade blocks our path. It is manned by neighbours. I recognise the man who gave O the tub of yoghurt at the cook-in, and the Sandal Man. C has O in his arms, as the men hurry us through a space around the side of the barricade. V scoops up E, even though her eyes are streaming and she must hardly be able to see where she is heading.

'They lied,' she says. 'To take us by surprise. Just like before.'

'Before?' I say.

She looks at me like I am stupid. 'Before here. When the soldiers came. The army. The Guards.'

V tightens her grip on E, as if he is her own brother, and runs with him through the mud. 'Come on!'

Behind us, the bulldozers rumble and growl.

Their barricade lasts for about thirty seconds. We stand away from it on the mud path as dust and dirt float up around us. Some of the men from the barricade have picked up rocks to throw at the bulldozers. They are charged by the Guards and clubbed to the ground.

'What about *our* home?' says L.

The shed? It's hardly a home. But in it is everything we own. I slump to the mud. Does it matter? What do I own? None of us even have a Life Book. I have a photo, of my mother and father, and my sisters and brothers, but it is in my pocket, where I always keep it, safe.

But L and E have their family album, full of pictures.

'Our album,' says L.

Their album is in the shed.

'Come on!' L yells.

As if I'd let her go on her own.

We leave E in V's arms, safe on the main pathway. I hate to leave him, and I hate the idea of running *into* the destruction and fighting, but I have no choice. L is already three steps ahead of me. We have to try and save our shack.

We run around the Guards, who are trying to round everybody up. In the heart of the Camp, if people stand still for long enough, the Guards come at them with their clubs and herd them into one spot, where they surround them. Nobody is allowed out. People who try to break out are sprayed with the tear gas. Some of the people are crying, some of the people are shouting angrily, and some of the people stand silent and sad.

We keep moving.

A group of men have built a burning barricade from some of the smashed-up shacks, and have armed themselves with sticks and rocks, which they are throwing at the Guards.

A big metal truck roars up with a bazooka on top. A Guard aims the bazooka at the men at the barricade. A jet of water fires out. The water knocks the men clean off their feet. The water-bazooka spurts across the burning barricade, extinguishing the flames and the men.

There are more Guards than usual. They have come from outside the Camp and have helmets with visors and big boots and plastic shields. Some of the men they strike with the shields, gashing their heads, smashing them to the ground. Then they drag them away.

L and I are coughing and spluttering. It is hard to see through all the smoke and the gas. It is hard to tell if the gas is tear gas or smoke from the burning shacks and barricades. It is hard to know which direction to run. We keep moving.

The mud drags at our ankles, trying to pull us down. Through the yelling, the crackle of flames and the clunk of rocks, I hear the warning *clatter* of the stork.

But the smoke clears, and in front of us is a Guard dressed in riot gear, and in his hands is a rifle, and the rifle is aimed at us.

This is just like it was at home. When they

bombed our houses and killed our neighbours. It is exactly like home.

L gives me a huge shove and I fall sideways into a pile of trash. She dives on top of me. I feel a whoosh of air going past my ears, and hear the *thunk thunk thunk* of bullets pelting into the mountain of rubbish next to us.

L's face is up close, in my face. She looks me in the eye. 'It's okay,' she's says. 'Rubber bullets. Only rubber bullets. They will not kill.'

Only rubber bullets. Okay.

We dig ourselves into the pile of rubbish. We burrow like *voles*. We tunnel through dirty clothes, abandoned tents, ashy sleeping bags and discarded bones. Through rolls of tarpaulin lined with pizza boxes, sour cartons, mouldy pans and a thousand pieces of smashed glass. The remains of other people's temporary shelters. We dig ourselves in, like animals gone to ground.

Boom boom boom go the bombs inside my heart. I tell myself to breathe easy, to take long, slow breaths, to relax. Don't panic. I tell myself it is just another game. A game of hide-and-seek.

In the dark, we scramble through the mountain of junk, feeling our way deeper into stuff that is so rubbish even people like us throw it away.

But the deeper we dig in, the further we are from the range of the bullets.

L stops, and I wiggle up next to her. I hear her panting – fast, panicked breath. The Guards will hear us! I put a finger to her lips, and try to slow my own breathing. Be still, be silent.

I count, to try and calm myself. *One ... two ... three ... four ...*

But I feel L trembling against me. I feel myself trembling. I feel the rubbish *clank* and *clunk* and *clatter* as it shifts and settles around us.

... twenty-three ... twenty-four ... twenty-five ... twenty-six ...

And a low growl.

The rubbish clamps itself around us, jabbing my back, forcing my head sideways, twisting my leg.

... sixty-one ... sixty-two ...

L gasps. The low growl builds into a thundering roar, like a beast at our backs, and I know it is the bulldozer come for us, sweeping the rubbish into its metal jaws.

Over the sound of the bulldozer's thunder, my heart goes *boom boom boom* and my head counts its calming rota of numbers.

. . . ninety-eight . . . ninety-nine . . . a hundred.

Coming! Ready or not!

I pull myself closer to L and we hold each other, as tight and as tiny as we can make ourselves. I squeeze my eyes shut, and try to block out the bulldozer's roar.

Who wants to play, I say to myself over and over. *Who wants to play?*

*

We stay buried for hours, our arms tightly round each other.

Finally, everything is still, and silent. I wiggle my toes, my fingers. I trace the curve of L's skull and feel that it is whole and round and uncracked. We breathe. We each let out a laugh, short, and unfunny. We push and wiggle ourselves some elbow space. Is it safe for us to show our faces? I do not want to be shot.

The bulldozer has passed us by, rolled its flattening way through to the edge of the Camp.

We dig ourselves out and blink in the daylight.

Everything has been flattened. Flattened or burnt. There are a few people wandering around in shock. There are some Guards too, yelling orders at people and kicking at the crap lying around in the mud.

L and I hold each other's hand as we make our way through the smoke. 'It's this way,' she says, but I do not know how she can tell, because there are none of the landmarks we usually use to make our way around Camp. The showers are gone, the school has been knocked down, most of the tents and shacks have been removed. The bulldozers and tractors are pummelling the last of them, finishing the job, clearing up.

After a while, L says, 'Here.'

There is nothing here. How can she tell?

But I see the sheet of corrugated plastic that used to be our window, flat on the ground, free from any frame. Tramped into the mud, the padlock to our door, still locked and fixed to its block of wood, smashed and pulled from the other bits of chipboard and plastic which was our door. I see the upturned crate we used as a table has been squashed flat, but all our stuff – a couple of plates, a towel, a glass jar, a piece of a mirror, a game of snakes and ladders – all gone.

Next to me, L is on her knees. She is digging a photo out of the mud, from her picture book. I see it is a picture of her, when she was younger, around E's age, and E, I suppose, when he was a baby, with two grown-ups I suppose were their mum and dad, smiling for the camera. L and E and their mum and dad as a whole family. We look and we look but there are no other pictures left.

*

We trudge our way up towards the women and children's centre, our bus, searching for E and the others. We pass the site of the youth club, just a bare patch now where it used to stand with its fresh-painted walls waiting for a roof.

Already I see some women digging through debris piled high on the side of the track. They pull out some lengths of cloth, some wire, a few sticks, a dented pan. They are going to start again. They wave at us as we pass. L calls out to them, asking if they have seen E, but they just shrug. They do not know E.

Further up the road, Ade has set up a stall made of old pallets and rocks, with a couple of his volunteers. They have made a sign, which reads 'Free Bread'.

A Guard comes up to Ade and makes shooing gestures with his club. Ade stands his ground and he and the Guard have a short argument. Ade has a phone, and he speaks into it, then he pushes it at the Guard's face, like he is inviting the Guard to speak into it. But the Guard shakes his head and hurries away. The Guard has lost the argument. Ade thrusts the phone back into his pocket, and shakes his own head and mutters to himself.

We stop and he offers us some bread. We shovel it down while we take in the destruction around us.

'What happened?' I ask.

Ade stares down at the ground. 'They said they wouldn't do it until next week.' He looks like he wants to spit. 'They said they wouldn't use force.'

'What?' I repeat. But Ade looks too angry to speak.

'Relocation,' says L. 'I heard talk of this, around the fires.'

Ade looks up. 'For your own good,' he says.

I laugh, despite myself. This is no time for jokes.

'The Camp was a danger to good health, a threat to life,' he says. 'The Guards say they have a responsibility towards your well-being.'

'So they smashed up our shack?'

'For your own good,' he repeats.

'But,' says L, 'where will we live now?'

Ade turns his face away. His mouth twists. He raises his arm and he points, all the way up the hill.

But all I see is the big metal boxes.

Today there are more of them than ever. Long oblong boxes. For carrying cargo. Over the top of the hill I see line after line of them, one after the other, and where there isn't enough space, piled one on top of the other.

I remember, again. I remember one morning when the bombers came to our village, and the bombs dropped. *Boom boom boom.* On our school. And afterwards, when the villagers had dug through the debris, our streets were filled with the sound of sobbing. There were so many coffins. Placed alongside each other. Long oblong boxes, like these, full of bodies.

We need to find Charity. Adrian says he thought he saw V and E heading towards the double-decker. L and I thank him for the bread, and we head off.

I wonder what will greet us when we get to the site of the children's centre. Will we see an empty patch of ground there as well, and Charity gone?

But before we make it there, we hear an engine running, a horn tooting. We see the red double-decker bobbing along the rutted mud track towards us. C is hanging out from one of the windows, taking our picture, and V is on the front seat on the upper deck, next to E. E is banging his fist on the window, to get our attention, waving at us.

The bus draws to a halt alongside us, and the doors pull open with a hiss. Charity is in the driving seat, and she turns and smiles at us.

'Hop aboard,' she says.

L, I, V, E

The bus is crammed full of children. The smell of hot coffee and a huge noise of excited chatter flow out from the open door. Charity and her helpers have been driving around, picking up all the waifs and strays. Everybody has a bun in one hand and a steaming plastic cup in the other.

At the back of the bus, some kids are playing a clapping game.

It is like another world.

E clatters down the stairs and wraps his arms

around L's waist. She ruffles his hair and kisses his head. 'It's all right,' she says. 'Everything is fine.'

Charity presses the button that closes the door behind us, and she climbs out of the driver's space.

'Come upstairs,' she says. 'V wants to show off her wound.'

V is on the front seat, propped up by cushions. She smiles when she sees us. E runs to her side.

'I was worried you guys had been hosed down,' she smiles. She holds her nose. 'But the smell tells me you haven't even been anywhere near water – for weeks.'

L moves forward to give her a hug. But V holds up her palm.

'Show them!' says E, his eyes wide with excitement.

V tugs at the neck of her top, tugging it aside, so we can see her shoulder. She has a red and purple bruise, as wide as a golf ball. It is all swollen up, as big as a golf ball too.

'Ouch,' I say.

'She got hit by a rubber bullet,' says Charity.

'She was a leaping lion!' says E. 'The Guard thought she was wild.'

'I almost got my teeth into him,' says V.

From nowhere, Charity has a giant bag of crisps in her hands. She rips the bag open. 'Snackeroos,' she says, 'for all my little lions.'

Before any of us can stop him, E shoves his face into the opened bag.

'Elvoi!' he declares, and makes snuffling sounds.

'Rarf rarf,' says V, managing a smile. She gently nudges E's head away from the packet. She holds out her palm in a *give* motion. He's got a zillion crisps dangling from his lips and he drops a mouthful into V's hand. She shoves them straight in her mouth.

'Gross,' says L.

V munches down the crisps, while C points his phone at her bruising and takes a picture. 'Good job it was only a rubber bullet,' says V, looking pointedly at E, who has his head stuck back in the crisps. 'Like a bouncy ball. Or a plastic puppet.'

'Or a paper plane,' I say. 'Or a twig pistol.'

Or a water cannon.

I notice Charity staring at us, one at a time, as if she is checking our faces. She glances up to the far end of the bus with a big frown. It reminds me of when I used to go to school and the teacher would do a head count.

To check. To check that everybody is safe and sound.

Except Charity's not counting heads – she is checking faces.

The sides of her mouth drop. She tells us all to sit down and listen.

We sit and Charity lets out a long sigh. 'Okay,' she says, 'I have to ask. And this is very important.'

We wait, silent.

And Charity says, 'Has anybody seen O?'

L and I look at each other in surprise.

O?

The last time I saw O was just before L and I ran off to try and save our shack. C had him.

I look at C.

He looks sheepish. 'I thought O went off with you guys,' he says. 'Then a Guard tried to snatch my phone because I was taking pictures. Then . . . then I tried to stop V from getting shot. And then, then . . .'

He trails off and closes his eyes. I feel sorry for him. It is not C's fault. He can't be responsible for looking after all of us.

'So,' says Charity. 'O was never with you two.'

She doesn't look at C, but I can tell she is disappointed in him. O is still just a toddler, isn't he? C is almost a man.

'Well, where is he then?' I ask. I realise it is a really unhelpful question. I want to kick myself.

'I know!' L perks up. 'It's obvious, isn't it?'

We all stare at her.

'The Play Tree!' she says. 'He'll be down by the Play Tree. He'll be waiting for us. Waiting for us to do the puppet game.'

'Eating berries!' yells E, still fingering the last of the crisp crumbs into his mouth.

I swear, you can feel the relief actually landing around our circle.

C looks at us. 'We'll go get him,' he says. 'We'll go get him, right now!'

The lot of us stand up straight away – even V, although her shoulder is obviously hurting at least an eight on a scale of one to ten. Everybody knows there is no point in telling her to sit down, and leave it to the rest of us.

'All right,' says Charity. She gives C the sternest of looks. 'But this time, make sure that you all stick together. No matter what.'

I recognise the look. It is the look my own mother used to give me when I was in charge of my little sisters on our journey to school. My heart cramps inside my chest. I gaze at Charity. *Give me that look*, I will her. *Give me that look.*

But she doesn't. Her gaze stays fixed on her own son, and it turns into a smile as Seymour replies, 'Don't worry, Mum – we will stick together, I promise.'

We will stick together. No matter what.

The whole Camp seems to be melting away to nothing. There are no tents left, no shacks remaining upright. No fires. No stalls. Just Guards, brushing the mud off their trousers, wiping their clubs clean, smoking their cigarettes even though this is not their smoking patch.

It *wasn't* their smoking patch. It was our space. But not any more. Now it is owned by the Guards. And the bulldozers.

The bulldozers are hard at work. They are clearing the ground. They are sweeping everything clean. Clearing away torn-off roofs, chopped up tables, discarded bedding, cinders of this, ashes of that. Bottles and bricks and books and footballs and phones. Everything.

The whole Camp is being brushed down the hill into Deep Ditch. All that remains is a flat, muddy wasteland. The sun comes out and shines on nothing.

'My colour,' says V, as we trudge through the glistening sludge. 'A field of gold.'

We get to Deep Ditch. I know this is the place where Deep Ditch is because of the curve of the hill. But Deep Ditch has gone. Everything is quite simply flat.

Of course Deep Ditch had long ago stopped being a ditch. It was a mountain of waste beside a valley of sludge.

But there is nothing here now. There is only further flattened wasteland. The bulldozers have been pushing, pushing, pushing everything down from the Camp into the meadow.

The fence with the gap that I walked through has gone as well. The hedgerows on the nearside of the meadow have also been bulldozed away. I have an awful feeling in my belly.

We walk further down, and the more we walk the more I see that where there was green there is now only brown, the wasteland spreading itself into fresh territory.

There is no sign of O.

At the far end of the meadow, by the Play Tree, I see the bulldozers hard at work.

L has a tight hold of E's hand. V is grimacing from her bullet wound as we make our way. C has his phone out, taking pictures of it all. Today, the meadow is quiet. There is an absence of buzz and birds.

We reach our tree just as the bulldozer is setting to work around it. I see that the men in the bulldozers are not meaning to flatten our tree, neither were they meaning to flatten the hedgerows or the flowers or the grass. They are just trying to get rid of the Camp. They are completing the flattening.

The mounds of mud and muck that the bulldozers have been sweeping down the meadow are clumped with our clothing, our bedding, our cooking.

V looks at me, and she laughs.

I get it. The more they try and wipe us out, the further they spread us.

The Play Tree gives out a crack as the bulldozer's claw heaves into its trunk, tears at its roots.

The tree begins to give. The branch over which is threaded our Leaf Book begins to break. The leaves bearing our names shiver and shake.

The tree topples and crashes to the ground. And the bulldozer barges forward. The teeth of the dozer rip at the threads of Charity's blanket that I had used to tie our stories together. Our leaves flutter free, floating for a moment between the tree and the earth.

I take a breath.

We are all blown away in the breeze.

Boom goes my heart.

But in my head, the word is *broom,* not boom. The bombs are *brooms.* These bulldozers are *brooms.* The soldiers, the Guards, each one of them a broom.

Broom.

Scattering us, like leaves. From one part of the world to another.

I flutters down into the mud.

L and E are caught in a gust.

For a moment, V is cradled in the crook of

the tree, trembling against the bark, then she drops and sinks into the mud.

And O is gone, a leaf among leaves.

We will never return home. There is no home.

The bulldozer shovels the mud over what remains of the torn-up leaves, along with all that is left of the busted puppets, the green, the blue, the red and the gold.

Night-time comes, and we all sleep on the bus.

Charity does not want us to speak to the Guards. She does not trust them. Most of the grown-ups, and some of the families, are being fingerprinted and herded into the metal containers. But the containers are full and so some people are being put onto coaches and driven to other camps, who knows where. Others are being taken to police stations. Everybody is being removed, but where to, nobody knows.

We are being scattered.

Charity says we are safer with her, for now. She says plans are in place. There are people who are fighting our corner.

I say I don't want our corner to be fought. I don't want more fighting.

She says she chose the wrong words and she is sorry.

Her son says we have people watching our backs. But I think, *Most of them are pointing guns.*

And E says, 'Where is O? Why isn't O sleeping on the bus with us? What happened to O?'

I start to say, *who wants to play?* But I am exhausted. I fall asleep.

In the morning there is more hot coffee and buns. There are lots of grown-ups milling around the bus, and a lot of chatter.

Charity sees that I am awake. She comes up to me and smiles. 'We are going to find O,' she says.

'Yeah?' I say.

'Yes.'

I do not believe her.

People on the bus are huddled in groups. The children are squealing and laughing as they point their fingers and ooh and aah at whatever is the focus of their huddle.

'We will find you a home,' says Charity. 'We will find you all a home. We'll never stop until we've done it, we'll never rest.'

But I am already too tired. I feel finished.

There is a journalist on the bus, and he is asking questions. The children are bouncing up and down around him, wanting to make themselves heard.

I call over the top of their heads. 'Has anybody seen O? Has anybody seen O?'

But nobody hears.

C comes up to me. He is gripping a pile of paper, and his hand is resting on the shoulder of a kid I haven't seen before, who smiles at me.

C says, 'This is U.' I glance at U.

I frown at them both. 'I'm not in the mood,' I tell U.

'Go on, U,' C says. 'Tell him. Tell him what you saw.'

Child U raises an arm and points out of the bus window, up towards the top of the Camp. 'The fence is down,' says U. 'And the Guards are all busy, putting everyone onto coaches, or clearing the smashed-up shacks, or levelling Deep Ditch.'

This is not news.

'People are sneaking through the gap in the fence,' U continues. 'They are leaving the Camp. Moving forwards.'

'Forwards,' repeats C, waving his paper

bundle in enthusiasm. I want to swat the paper out of his hands. But he turns his face back to U. 'Tell him,' he says to U.

'Well,' U says, 'I can't be certain, but I think I might have spotted O.'

What? Why didn't C say so to begin with? I spring to my feet.

C peels away the top sheet from his bundle of paper. He places it down in front of U.

U and I look down at the sheet of paper. 'I've printed off dozens of these,' explains C, with some pride.

At the top of the sheet, typed in big bold letters, are the words:

HAVE YOU SEEN CHILD O?

Beneath the words is a picture of O, which C took when we were all down at the Play Tree, just before the bulldozers came.

In the picture, O is standing beneath a branch of the tree with a big grin on his face. His fingers are reaching up, the tips touching the bright green leaf attached by the woollen strand from Charity's blanket. His fingers are brushing the letter O, written in berry juice. His name. His Leaf Book. His Life Book. His Passport. O's smile is so wide I can see his teeth.

C shows us the next sheet of paper. This one has a picture of O, sitting on V's shoulders.

HAVE YOU SEEN CHILD O?

'Are you sure it was him?' C and I both ask at the same time.

U nods. 'Yes. Yes, it is. It is him. This is the child I saw making his way through the hole in the fence.'

I feel like my chest is bursting. I gather everybody round.

'Quickly,' I say. 'I've got a game, a new game. Who wants to play?' L raises her hand, and so does E. V raises her hand as well, even though it makes her grimace in pain. Charity starts to smile, and then she raises her hand too.

'This is the best game we will ever play,' I say. My voice is getting stronger. Not wobbly, not like the way I feel inside. 'It is a game of hide-and-seek. We are looking for O, and we will carry on playing it until the game is complete. Will you play?'

V snatches one of the pictures from C. She holds it up so we can all see the picture of O's face. Her fingers stroke O's cheek. 'When we find O, we will have won the game,' she says.

'Yes,' I say. 'Yes!'

'But where will we look?' says E.

Nobody answers.

Then L says, 'We will look everywhere.'

She looks up from the pile of pictures of O's life. She stares up at the white space that surrounds us, and opens her arms to the sky. Everywhere.

Charity starts up the bus. 'Come on, then. Everyone hop on,' she calls. 'Let's find O. The breach in the fence is five minutes' drive, straight up this track.'

We all huddle around the driver's cabin, as Charity puts her foot down and the bus roars into life.

'Hold on tight,' she warns us as the bus rocks its way over the rutted mud track. The brown, rotten, stinky mud.

V takes my hand, gripping my fingers tightly. We peer out of the window as the Camp rattles past us. It is a wasteland now, nothing but bonfires smoking against the blue sky. All that remains of our homes. Guards, kicking and prodding their way through the rubbish, checking no sign of life has managed to hide from the bulldozers. O is not here.

We see stragglers struggling up the path, loaded down by possessions and the children they hoist onto their shoulders.

The bus grumbles and groans as we make our way up the hill. As we gaze through the window, white feathers from the stork seem to flutter down around us.

No, not feathers. Leaves.

No, not leaves from a tree, but leaves of paper. Paper on which is the face of our mud child, of O. Floating around us, from the blue sky down into the sludge, scattered from the top deck by C and our new friend, U.

Pictures of O.

O sat on a bucket.

O eating an apple.

O in Charity's arms.

O being questioned by a Guard.

O playing the puppet game.

O singing his song.

Have you seen Child O?

His Life Book.

In every picture, O is smiling.

I see the Sandal Man bend down and pick up one of the sheets of paper. He peers at the image on the page. He keeps peering at it.

HAVE YOU SEEN CHILD O?

The Sandal Man smiles at us and nods. He lifts his arm and points at the road ahead. He remembers O. His smile turns to a grin and he gestures at us. *Hurry, hurry.*

As we reach the top end of the Camp we see the gap in the fence, unguarded, open for anyone to go on through. The Camp is finished now. This is not our home any more.

The bus trundles through the gap. We leave the Camp.

The road ahead breaks into three different directions.

'Which way?' asks L. 'Which way would O have gone?' Her voice rises.

As V squeezes my fingers, I take L's hand with my free hand. 'There's only one way he would have gone,' I say. E hugs himself tightly against L's hip and looks up at me. *Which way?* his eyes ask.

'Forwards.' And I smile. 'O would always go forwards.'

And so that's what we do. We go forwards. For O.

We go forwards.

All the events described in this story are real events which have happened to real children in real camps across the world, in recent months. For the purpose of the story, the children's names have been changed to letters. What has happened to the children in these camps has been documented with film, photographs and oral evidence on a wide range of news sites and websites.

For further details about the children living in these camps, and how to help, visit:

www.refugee-action.org.uk
www.helprefugees.org.uk
www.savethechildren.org.uk

FABER & FABER

has published children's books since 1929. Some of our very first publications included *Old Possum's Book of Practical Cats* by T. S. Eliot starring the now world-famous Macavity, and *The Iron Man* by Ted Hughes. Our catalogue at the time said that 'it is by reading such books that children learn the difference between the shoddy and the genuine'. We still believe in the power of reading to transform children's lives.

First published in 2018 by Faber & Faber Limited, Bloomsbury House, 74–77 Great Russell Street, London, WC1B 3DA

Typeset by MRules

Printed by CPI Group (UK) Ltd, Croydon CR0 4YY

All rights reserved

Text © Steve Tasane, 2018

The right of Steve Tasane to be identified as author of this work has been asserted in accordance with Section 77 of the Copyright, Designs and Patents Act 1988

A CIP record for this book is available from the British Library

ISBN 978–0–571–33783–5

FSC
www.fsc.org
MIX
Paper from responsible sources
FSC® C101712

2 4 6 8 10 9 7 5 3

About the Author

Steve Tasane is the author of two novels for young adults, *Blood Donors*, included on the Diverse Voices list of best 50 children's books celebrating cultural diversity, and *Nobody Saw No One*, selected as one of *The Guardian*'s Children's Books of the Year. He is also a performance poet who has featured at events ranging from Glastonbury Festival to Battersea Dogs Home and at hundreds of schools around the UK.

For my mother, Olive Tasane (1934–2018)